FRYDERYK

FANTA

BERCEUSE

BARCAROLLE

FRYDERYK CHOPIN
COMPLETE WORKS

ACCORDING
TO THE AUTOGRAPHS AND ORIGINAL EDITIONS
WITH A CRITICAL COMMENTARY

EDITOR
IGNACY J. PADEREWSKI
ASSISTED BY
LUDWIK BRONARSKI
AND
JÓZEF TURCZYŃSKI

WITH REPRODUCTIONS OF
PORTRAITS
AND MANUSCRIPTS

MCMXLIX

THE FRYDERYK CHOPIN INSTITUTE
POLSKIE WYDAWNICTWO MUZYCZNE

FRYDERYK CHOPIN
COMPLETE WORKS

XI

FANTASIA
BERCEUSE
BARCAROLLE

FOR PIANO

EDITORIAL COMMITTEE
I. J. PADEREWSKI
L. BRONARSKI
J. TURCZYŃSKI

TWENTY-SEVENTH EDITION

INSTYTUT FRYDERYKA CHOPINA
POLSKIE WYDAWNICTWO MUZYCZNE

COVER AND LAY-OUT – LUDWIK GARDOWSKI

MUSIC MATRICES PRODUCED
BY POLSKIE WYDAWNICTWO MUZYCZNE
TEXT SET IN PÓŁTAWSKI 'ANTIQUA' TYPE
PRINTED IN POLAND 2017
ISMN 979-0-2740-0178-0

I. A. BISSON – PHOTOGRAPH OF CHOPIN c. 1849

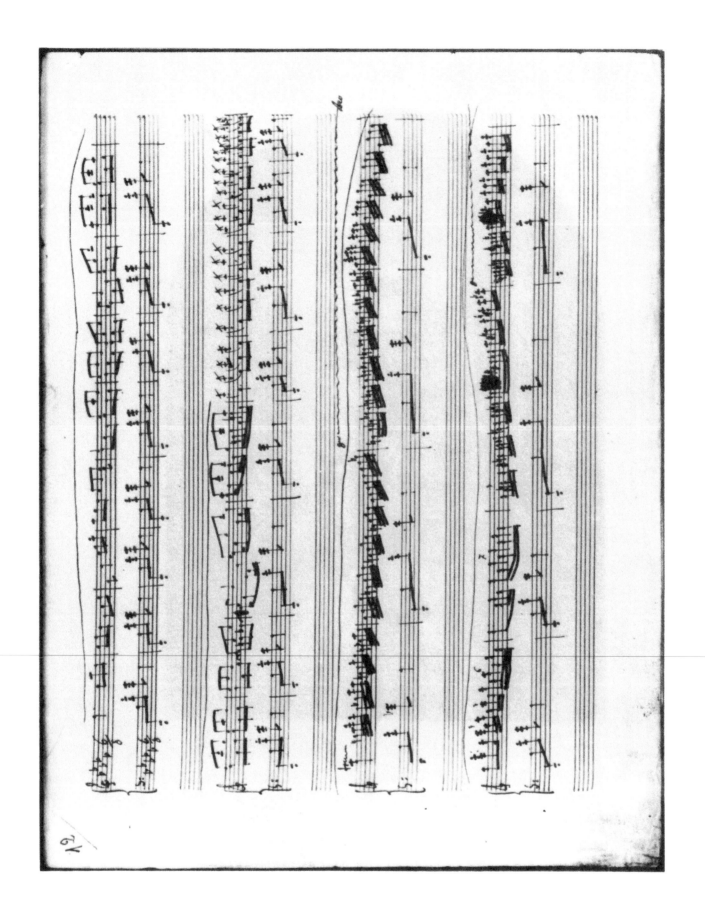

AUTOGRAPH OF THE BERCEUSE (P. 1)

AUTOGRAPH OF THE BERCEUSE (P. 2)

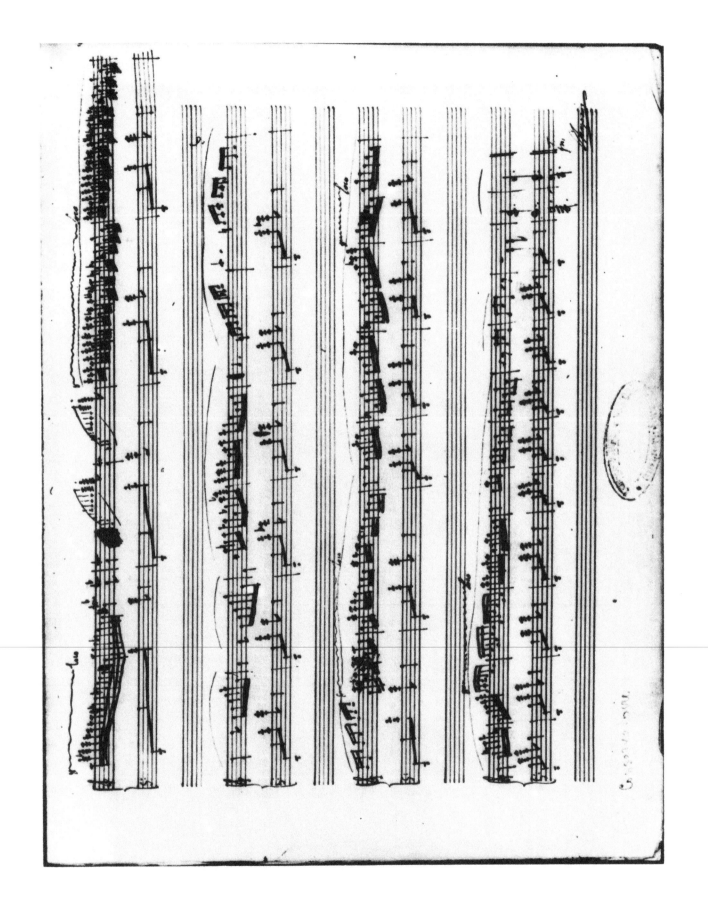

AUTOGRAPH OF THE BERCEUSE (P. 3)

FANTAISIE

BERCEUSE

BARCAROLLE

A Madame la Princesse C. de Souzzo

FANTAISIE

FR. CHOPIN
Op. 49

Ped. *come sopra*

A Mademoiselle Elise Gavard

BERCEUSE

Op.57

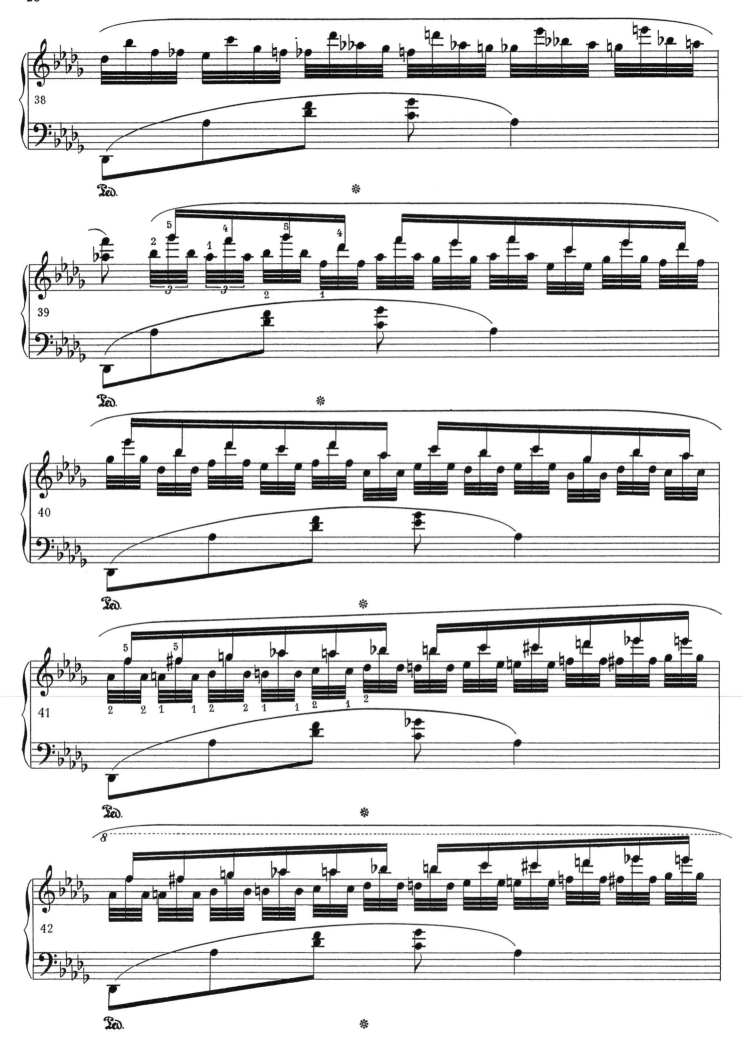

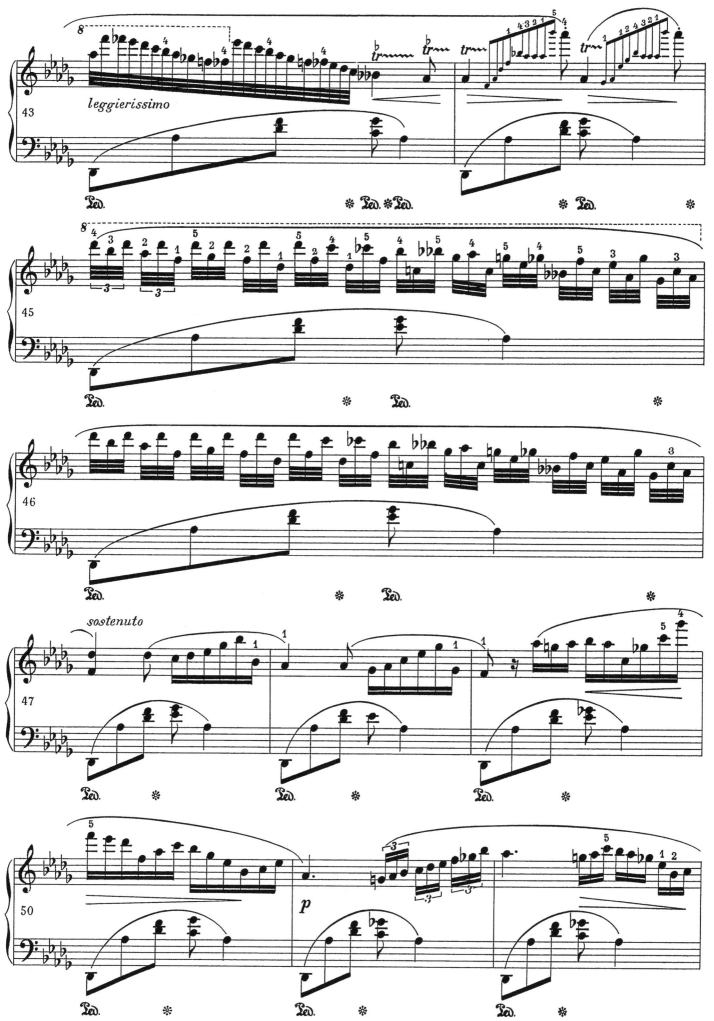

A Madame la Baronne de Stockhausen

BARCAROLLE

Op. 60

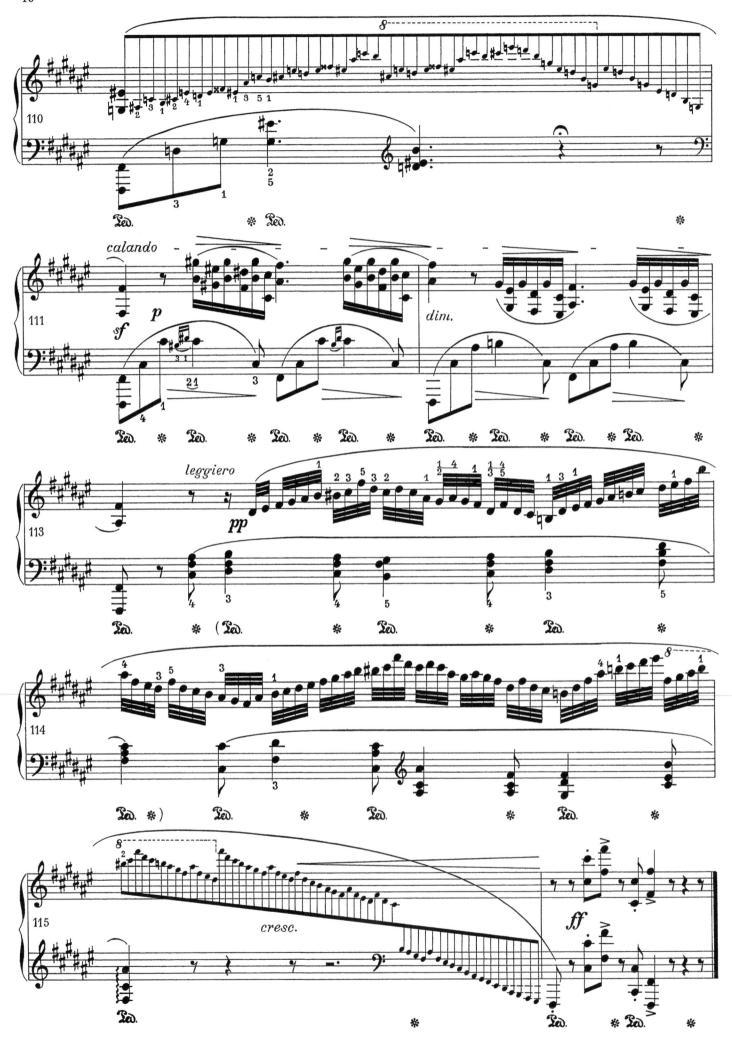

THE CHARACTER OF THE PRESENT EDITION

The principal aim of the Editorial Committee has been to establish a text which fully reveals Chopin's thought and corresponds to his intentions as closely as possible. For this reason the present edition has been based primarily on Chopin's autograph manuscripts, copies approved by him, and first editions. The Committee has had to take into account the fact that even though a manuscript may have served as a basis for a first edition, it is not always the final version of any particular piece. Chopin frequently changed details of his compositions up to the very last moment. So much is clear not only from contemporary sources, but also from variants between original editions and manuscripts. Such variants, moreover, cannot possibly be considered to be engraver's errors or editorial alterations. The manuscripts will always be the prime source for the textual verification of Chopin's works. But although no effort has been spared, it has not always been possible to discover or study a given manuscript. The Editorial Committee has also consulted recent editions for purposes of comparison.

When it has proved impossible to establish the authentic version or the one corresponding to Chopin's last intentions, any discrepancy has been carefully indicated in the Commentary.

Dynamic and agogic signs correspond to the manuscripts and first editions. Sometimes they have been supplemented by the repetition of signs appearing in identical or similar places. Other additions have been placed in brackets. Chopin's original fingering, rare though it is in the manuscripts and first editions, has been expressly indicated in the Commentary.

The pedal marks given by the Editorial Committee are strictly in accordance with the manuscripts and original editions. Certain insignificant modifications have been introduced, but only where this is required by the greater resonance of modern pianos, as well as in analogous passages or repetitions, where comparison has revealed inconsistency, or where correction or completion is required owing to mistakes or negligence. Chopin's pedal-marking is usually careful, precise, and in certain places very delicate, sometimes producing entirely new pianistic effects (e.g. at the beginning of the Polonaise-Fantasia). Those passages in which Chopin has not marked the pedalling are generally explained by the fact that the pedalling required is very simple, and is therefore self-evident; or, on the contrary, that it is so subtle as to be too complicated, if not impossible, to indicate. In any case, the use of the pedal is a very delicate and entirely individual matter, depending on many factors, such as instrument, touch, tempo or acoustics of the room. For this reason, the Editorial Committee has decided to leave the pedalling as found in the original documents. This conforms with the principles adopted in the present edition.

In principle, Chopin's phrasing has been retained. But certain slurs have been modified in the interests of simplicity, exactitude or clarity. In Chopin's manuscripts slurs are sometimes placed carelessly, and do not always correspond in original editions.

The editors have introduced some slight modifications of the original in the arrangement and outward appearance of the musical text. Harmonic notation and accidental signs have been altered or added where necessary, and certain changes in the distribution of notes have been effected so as to ensure the clearest visual presentation of the music, of the composer's intentions, and to safeguard the performer from hesitations, uncertainties or misunderstandings. In these cases, the editors have endeavoured to keep to the notation of the manuscripts and first editions as closely as possible, and have tried to avoid the exaggerations which sometimes characterize previous editions of Chopin's works.

For this reason also, we have very often left certain inconsistencies occurring in the notation of similar passages undisturbed. Such variants often appear in Chopin's works, not only in the notation but also in the contents of the music. Any important modification of Chopin's notation, however, has been clearly indicated in the Commentary.

In ornamentation, Chopin's original notation has been retained; attention has been drawn to any ornament appearing in different forms in the manuscripts and original editions. Wherever the execution of an ornament may give rise to doubt, the most appropriate manner has been carefully shown.

The chief difficulty lies in the method of beginning a trill. The following principles should be observed:

1) Where the principal note of a trill is preceded by an upper appoggiatura: [musical notation], or by a sequence of grace notes: [musical notation], the trill begins on the upper note: [musical notation]. In the latter case ([musical notation]), the repetition of the principal note at the beginning should be avoided.

The following: [musical notation] does not exist in Chopin. To obviate this mistake certain editors have added an upper appoggiatura to the notation of these trills: [musical notation]

2) Where the principal note of the trill is preceded by the same note written as an appoggiatura:

, the trill should always begin on the principal

note: , but should never be played thus:

etc.

3) Doubt may arise where the notation of the trill contains no appoggiatura. In his study *Ornamentation in the Works of Fred. Chopin* (London 1921, p. 1), J. P. Dunn suggests that in these cases the trill should always begin on the principal note (as if it were

written:).

Contrary to the opinion often expressed that a trill should always begin on the upper note, this principle is confirmed by the fact that Chopin sometimes writes a trill with an appoggiatura on the same pitch level as the principal note, and at other times, in a similar or corresponding place, completely omits the appoggiatura, and *vice-versa*; e. g. in the autograph of the first movement of the Sonata in B minor the trill in bar 52 is written without an appoggiatura, while the corresponding trill in the recapitulation has, in addition to the principal note, an appoggiatura on the same pitch level. There is no reason whatsoever to suppose that the second trill should be executed differently from the first.

Dunn adds (op. cit., p. 24) that the trills written without the principal note given as an appoggiatura may sometimes begin on the upper note, where this does not disturb the melodic line. Generally speaking, it can be established as a principle that in doubtful cases the trill should be started so as to link up as smoothly as possible with the preceding notes, e. g. filling a missing step or avoiding the repetition of a principal note, already performed (cf. ex. 1 and 2).

4) Difficulty may arise from the fact that Chopin sometimes used *tr* in place of the conventional sign to indicate a mordent. In the autograph MS of the Ballade

in A♭ major a simple mordent sign appears in bar 3, while at the corresponding point in bar 39 Chopin has written *tr* (see also Bronisława Wójcik-Keuprulian *Melodyka Chopina*, Lwów 1930, p. 56). This is justifiable in so far as the mordent is a short form of the trill, and in a quick movement the trill is often executed as a mordent. Places where the *tr* sign may be taken to be a mordent have been indicated in the Commentary.

5) When the ending of a trill is not expressly indicated, the trill should always be completed by playing the principal note after the upper note.

6) Finally, it must be remembered that all ornaments, whether appoggiaturas, mordents, trills, turns or arpeggios, should be performed according to the accepted principle, i. e. the duration of the ornament must be subtracted from the duration of the principal

note, e. g.: is played:

or

In Chopin's works, the signs written in his own hand in the copies of Madame Dubois, now preserved in the Library of the Paris Conservatoire (see E. Ganche *Dans le souvenir de Fr. Chopin*, Paris 1925, p. 205 et seq.), leave no doubt, from the rhythmic point of view, as to Chopin's method of executing these ornaments. There, *inter alia*, we find signs indicating that the first note of the ornament in the upper staff is to be played simultaneously with the bass note corresponding to the principal note of the ornament, e. g. in Nocturne op. 37 No. 1, and in Study op. 10 No. 3:

In this last case, the $G\sharp^1$ of the appoggiatura should be played simultaneously not only with the E in the bass, but also with the lower $G\sharp$ in the treble.

COMMENTARY

Fantasia in F minor, op. 49

Abbreviations: FE — the original French edition (M. Schlesinger, Paris, No. 3489). BE — the edition by Breitkopf & Härtel, Leipzig (collected edition, vol. X, No. 7); in general this is the same as Breitkopf & Härtel's original edition. ME — Mikuli's edition (F. Kistner, Leipzig, No. 5360—5362). In addition, the editions of Klindworth (Bote & Bock, Berlin), L. Köhler (Litolff, Brunswick), E. Sauer (B. Schotts Söhne, Mainz) and A. Casella (Curci, Naples) have been collated.

Bar *1*. BE gives the tempo as *Marcia, Grave.* The original version does not slur the first octave *F* to the following *C*, even placing a *staccato* dot over the *F*'s. Köhler, Sauer and Casella have slurs here, by analogy with later repetitions of the motive:

Bar *10*. In the chord on the third beat, FE lacks $E\flat^1$ and $A\flat^1$, and the top note, C^2, is not tied either back or forward. But in the copy belonging to Chopin's sister, Madame Jędrzejewicz, these ties and an $A\flat^1$ have been added in pencil. As BE does not have the C^2, it also has no ties; the $E\flat^1$ is also absent. ME has the full chord, but ties the C^2 only to the following C^2.

Bars *15—16*. FE, BE and ME do not have octaves in the left hand, but only the upper notes, as in bars 1—2. Chopin did not add lower octaves, in contrast to bars 11—12, probably because the bottom $_1C\flat$ was not available. The octaves added in some recent editions (Klindworth, Sauer, Casella) in bars 15 and 16, by analogy with bars 11—12, seem to be justified, and so we have accepted them.

Bars *19—20*. FE has no ties between the last chord of bar 19 and the first of bar 20. BE and ME tie only the $D\flat^1$. We have also accepted the tying of the $G\flat^1$, as found in Klindworth's and Köhler's editions.

Bar *25*. In contrast to the corresponding bars 33 and 34, on the second beat of the bar in the left hand, FE, BE and ME have not only the fifth $D\flat$-$A\flat$ but also the lower $A\flat$; the same applies to bar 26. Following other editions we have here reproduced the version of bars 33 and 34, which is less heavy and sounds better.

Bars *26* and *34*. For the last crotchet in the left hand BE gives $A\flat$-$E\flat$-$A\flat$, i.e. the same chord as at the end of the preceding bar.

Bar *27*. FE and ME do not have C^1 in the last chord in the left hand; however, they do have it in the corresponding bar 35.

Bar *28*. In FE the grace note C^2 is not tied to the following C^2; the same applies to bar 36. We have accepted the version of ME and BE. The last note in the treble, A^1, is not tied in FE or BE, or in ME, and we have accepted this version. It is, however, probable that both these notes should be tied; this is suggested by the accent on the last A^1. Casella has such a tie.

Bars *43—59*. In this passage the editors give two fingerings. Some (Mikuli, Köhler, Sauer) give the left hand for the first three notes of bars 43, 45, 47 etc. — with the fingering 5 1 5 2, after which they continue with the right hand, 1 2 4 3 etc. Others (Klindworth, Casella) divide this phrase between the hands as follows:

i.e. the right hand enters on the third note of the phrase, to be intercepted by the left hand. This last fingering accords better with the phrasing and enables the motives to be better emphasized. Though all four quaver triplets form a continuous melodic line, the first two notes are really only the foundation, and the theme itself begins on the third note:

This is indicated not only by the rests at the beginning of bars 43 and 54, but also by the upward quaver tails added to the third notes of these bars. Again, this motive is repeated very frequently throughout the work, in altered rhythm and shortened, but always with the characteristic leap of the fourth at the beginning (see bar 143 sqq., bar 180 sqq., bar 223 sqq., etc.). The slurring in bar 43 and the following bars is careless and inconsistent in FE (in bars 43, 45, 49 and 50 the slurs start at the beginning of the bar, in bars 47 and 48 on the fourth quaver; bars 54—55 and 56—57 have single slurs, and in bar 58 the slur starts at the beginning of the bar and carries on over the beginning of bar 59, where a new one begins on the fourth note). BE always starts the slurs at the beginnings of the bars containing quavers; and this slurring is followed here.

Bar *54*. FE lacks the crotchet rest at the beginning of the bar, but has it in the corresponding bar 43. BE and ME give it in both passages.

Bar *55*. FE lacks the $E\flat$ in the chord.

Bar *61*. The fingering 1 2 for the eighth and ninth quavers is found in both FE and BE.

Bars *64–67*. In the notation of the chord in these bars Klindworth changes the *Cb* to *B*. In view of the resolution in bar 68 to *C-E-G*, i.e. to the dominant in F minor, this is correct, since *B-Db-F-Ab* is the subdominant seventh in F minor with sharpened root. Since, however, the chord might at first be understood as the dominant seventh of *Gb* major, we have for the sake of simplicity left the original notation.

Bar *68*. FE does not mark *agitato*. The pedal is given only in the first half of the bar, and in bar 69 not at all, as in the corresponding bars 235–236. In bars 155–156 the pedal is marked only in the second half of bar 156. BE marks the pedal for the whole of bar 68, for the third beat of bar 69 and for the whole of bar 155; there are two pedal marks in bar 156, and in bar 235 one pedal for the first three beats and a second on the fourth beat; there are, however, two pedals in bar 236.

Bars *72–73*. FE and ME tie the *F¹*; however, they do not tie the corresponding note at bars 159–160 or 239–240.

Bars *77–84*. In this passage and its later repetitions FE marks no dynamics and BE has only the *crescendo* signs in bars 81, 84, 164, 168 and 244. The first question that arises is how each of these three passages should be begun. They are preceded each time by a *crescendo* which lasts through several bars. It would seem that the passage in bar 77 and the following bars, with their subsequent repetitions, should be begun *forte*. Recent editions (except Mikuli's, which gives no indications), however, indicate *piano* and *dolce*. This dynamic shade is more appropriate to the high register of the first four bars of· these passages, but we suggest that the following four bars, which are a repetition in a lower register, should be played with a mounting *crescendo*.

Bars *78, 80* and *82*. In these bars the notation of the last triplet in the right hand, or rather of the voice under it, merits attention. In FE both notes in question, i.e. Ab^2-Bb^2, Gb^1-Bb^1 and Ab^1-Bb^1 respectively, are quavers; but the Bb^2 or Bb^1 is placed, in bars 78 and 82, immediately beneath the third quaver of the triplet, while in bar 80 it lies between the second and third notes of the triplet. The corresponding notes in the passage at bar 164 sqq. are given in FE once under the first and third notes of the triplet, but twice (bars 167 and 169) the second of them is placed between the second and third notes of the triplet. In bars 245, 247 and 249, FE notates the Db^3, C^2 and Db^2 as dotted quavers, and the Eb^3 or Eb^2 as a semiquaver placed beneath the third note of the corresponding triplet. This notation is found in BE in all the nine passages mentioned. However Mikuli, in the first six cases, always places the second of the lower quavers between the second and third notes of the triplet; in the last three cases he follows FE's notation, but places the second note, i.e. the semiquaver, after the triplet. Recent editions accept the simultaneous playing of these notes, notating the lower voice in quavers (Klindworth, Köhler) or as crotchet+quaver (Sauer). Casella writes the notes in question as quavers, but in the way that FE does in bars 78–82, i.e. placing the second of the two lower notes under the third note of the triplet in bars 78 and 82, and between the second and third notes of the triplet in bar 80. Casella then repeats this notation exactly in bars 165–169 and 245–249; thus he accepts a polyrhythmic execution in bars 80, 167 and 247. But as all these notations, despite their differences, certainly – especially in view of the quick tempo – mean the same, i'e. the simultaneous playing of the last notes of both voices, we have made the notation uniform, accepting that used by Klindworth and Köhler in their editions.

Bar *81*. The original notation gives Eb^1 as the eighth quaver in the bass. We accept the change to *Db*, introduced by Klindworth by analogy with bar 168, for the sake of the stepwise progression of the top notes of the left-hand figures.

Bars *85–86 and similar bars*. Following Klindworth we have added a downward crotchet tail to the seventh quaver in the treble in order to indicate that it is the resolution of the top note of the left-hand chord at the beginning of the bar. The slurs linking the two notes have been reproduced from BE.

Bars *95–96*. BE slurs the triplet on the second beat of the bar with the following one, the triplet on the fourth beat with the first of the following bar, etc., as far as the first note in bar 97. The same notation is found in bars 99–100, but in the corresponding bars 262–264 and 266–267 both BE and FE have the same slurring as is given here.

Bars *101–109*. The long slurs have been added by us. In bar 101 the *p* is taken from ME.

Bars *109–126*. In these bars FE marks the pedal only in bar 112 (beginning on the minim), bar 114 throughout the first three beats, bars 119–123 with a change at the minim in bar 121 and ending after the first chord of bar 123. In the corresponding passage at bar 276 sqq. FE marks the pedal for the first three beats of bars 277, 279, 281, 283, for the last three beats of bars 284 and 285, and then one pedal in bars 286–288 (until the rest) and in bar 288 (from the minim) to the end of bar 290.

Bars *111, 113, 115, 117, 118, 119*. The original version gives the first chords of all these bars as crotchets with *staccato* dots, while the corresponding chords at bar 276 sqq. are quavers with a quaver rest. We have left this difference in the notation. The execution is the same in both cases.

44

Bars *112* and *116*. Though FE, BE and even ME have the octave $_1E\flat$-$E\flat$ in the bass at the beginnings of these bars (as in bars 110 and 114), we have accepted the change introduced in recent editions by analogy with bars 279 and 283. It ts obvious that only the range of the contemporary keyboard compelled Chopin to modify the more appropriate version.

Bar *113.* At the beginning of the bar in the bass we have kept the octave $E\flat$-$E\flat$ from the original version, though we consider that the fifth ($E\flat$-$B\flat$), as found in the corresponding bar 280, would be more appropriate.

Bar *117*. FE, BE and ME have an $E\flat$ at the beginning of the bar in the left hand in addition to the fifth $E\flat$-$B\flat$. We have accepted the version of the more recent editions.

Bar *122*. FE has no E^1 at the beginning of the bar.

Bar *123*. Following Klindworth, we have added to the second chord in the left hand a $G\sharp$ which is not found in the original version, but which gives the chord a fuller sound — more appropriate at this climactic point — and a form better suited to the subsequent harmonic progression.

Bar *124*. *Stretto* is added according to BE, which has this indication at the corresponding bar 291.

Bars *127–142*. FE and BE do not mark the pedal either in this passage or in the similar bars 294–309.

Bar *130*. FE and BE do not have the F in the last chord in the right hand, though it is present in bar 138.

Bar *172*. FE and ME do not have *forte* in bar 172 or *crescendo* in bar 178. We have reproduced these indications from BE.

Bar *175*. BE and ME have F and not $D\flat$ as the last quaver of the bar. From the notation in these editions as well as from that of FE, which gives $D\flat$, we may conclude that this last quaver should be played with the right hand.

Bar *180*. *Piano* is reproduced from ME. The $B\flat$, which is played with the right hand, should be intercepted by the left hand; the same applies to bar 184. In bars 182 and 186 this $B\flat$ can even be played simultaneously with the first finger of the right hand and the second of the left.

Bars *182–198*. Here FE has a different pedalling. In bar 182 it marks the pedal as early as the third beat of the bar, in bar 184 from the second beat until the beginning of bar 186, then a new pedal on the second beat of bar 186, lifted on the third beat of bar 187. The pedal is then marked under the last note in bar 187, but no lifting is marked. BE marks the pedal on the third beat of bars 182, 184 and 186 and indicates that it should be held throughout the following bar. In bar 188 the pedal mark is given under the third beat of the bar, but there is no indication as to how long it should be held.

Bar *186*. BE has $_1E\flat$ (as a crotchet) under the fifth $E\flat$-$B\flat$ (as minims) here but not in bar 184.

Bar *195*. BE has $B\flat$ and not $G\flat$ as the lowest note of both chords is the left hand.

Bars *199–205*. In FE, these bars have a single slur, as in bars 207–215.

Bars *199–222*. Throughout the whole *Lento* section FE has no pedalling. BE marks the pedal in bars 199 and 222, and in bar 215 prolongs it until the second beat of bar 216.

Bar *208*. In the original notation, the first chord of the bar appears only in three voices and so, in this harmonic progression, is apparently incomplete. Klindworth, Köhler and Sauer complete it by repeating the E^1 from the preceding chord. We consider, however, that the E^1 at the end of bar 207 should be seen as leading to the $C\sharp^1$ at the beginning of bar 208; we have therefore added an upward crotchet tail to the $C\sharp$ — which appears in the tenor voice — in order to emphasize the alto voice.

Bar *209*. In the last chord the original notation has A^1 and not $G\sharp\sharp^1$. This chord is the subdominant with added sixth in $D\sharp$ minor, with root raised from $G\sharp$ to $G\sharp\sharp$ and leading to $A\sharp$ in the dominant chord in the same key.

Bars *210–211*. FE does not tie the sixth E^1-$C\sharp^2$. We have accepted the version of ME and BE.

Bar *220*. Neither FE nor ME have the G^1, the passing note between $G\sharp^1$ and $F\sharp^1$. We reproduce it from BE.

Bar *221*. In recent editions not only the $C\sharp^1$ but also the E^1 is tied in the last two chords.

Bar *235*. In contrast to the corresponding octave in bar 155, FE and BE here give the first octave in the bass as a quaver followed by a quaver rest.

Bar *238*. FE does not break the slur, either here or at bars 240 and 241.

Bar *244*. FE and ME have $A\flat^1$ as the fifth quaver in the bass. We have accepted BE's version in view of the stepwise movement of the top notes of the figures (F^1-$G\flat^1$-$A\flat^1$-A^1-$D\flat^2$).

Bar *251*. As the third quaver in the treble FE has — apparently by mistake — not the sixth F^1-$D\flat^2$ but the octave $D\flat^1$-$D\flat^2$.

Bars *252–254*. Casella considers that the left hand of these bars is, erroneously, incomplete; he completes it as follows:

We do not think, however, that this omission was unintentional. It is much more probable that Chopin did not want such heavy chords in so low a register.

Bar *266*. At the beginning of the bar in the treble FE and ME have only the octave C^2-C^3.

Bars *275* and *276*. In the right hand of bar 275 we have added a crotchet tail to the last $E\flat^2$ and tied it to the following bar, by analogy with bars 108—109.

Bars *294 sqq. Più mosso* is found in BE and ME. BE has *sempre forte. Sempre più mosso* is found in BE at bars 306—307. ME gives this indication as early as bar 302, where BE has *cresc.* FE lacks all these indications. In bar 310 only BE has *ff*.

Bar *321*. FE does not indicate *smorzando*. BE has no arpeggio sign before the last chord.

Bar *322*. FE and ME do not mark *alla breve*. They give only one pedal, from the beginning of this bar until the beginning of bar 330.

Berceuse in D♭ major, op. 57

Abbreviations: FE — the original French edition (J. Meissonnier, Paris; MS — the autograph in the Library of the Paris Conservatoire according to the facsimile published at the beginning of the second volume of the Oxford edition of Chopin's works (Oxford University Press); this edition is denoted by OE. The rough drafts are from the reproduction in *Trois manuscrits de Chopin* (published by Dorbon aîné, Paris). In his comments on these reproductions Alfred Cortot discussed the differences between the original version, as represented in the rough drafts, and the final version.

Bars *1—2*. These bars are missing both in the rough drafts and in MS.

Bar *5*. OE has the fingering 2 $\overset{\frown}{42}$ $\overset{\frown}{32}$ for the first three notes in the treble.

Bar *7*. Though the original version does not break the slur at the beginning of the bar, we start a new slur here to emphasize the beginning of a new passage, i.e. the first variation of the theme. At the beginning of bar 11, where a new variation begins, we do not break the slur because, owing to the ingenious development of the melodic line, both variations are so intimately connected that the beginning of the new one comes almost imperceptibly. Klindworth very rightly stresses in his notation the F^2 at the beginning of bar 11 which, as the first note of the theme, should be brought well into prominence here as well.

Bar *12*. The fingering of the last two lower notes in the right hand is taken from OE.

Bar *13*. OE gives the first finger for the first three notes in the lower voice in the right hand (after the tied $G\flat^1$), and 2 1 2 for the last three notes (see *Appendix* below).

Bar *14*. The $G\flat^2$ at the beginning of the bar is not tied in either MS or FE, but it is tied in Mikuli's edition and in the majority of recent editions, by analogy with the G^1 at bars 12—13. It is worth noting, however, that the tie at bars 12—13, as found in the rough draft, was at first marked by Chopin in

MS as well, but then crossed out, i.e. he wanted to make it correspond to the untied $G\flat^2$'s in bars 13—14 (see *Appendix* below).

Bars *15—18*. There is no doubt that the grace notes, containing the theme, should be played simultaneously with the notes in the left hand; it follows that the repeated lower $A\flat^1$'s in the right hand come slightly late. The true rhythm would emerge more clearly from the following notation:

The complexity of such a notation, however, would present difficulties of reading and comprehension. Chopin, who always tried to use the simplest and clearest notation — the easiest both to write and read — has done so here; his version should be regarded as the most appropriate.

Bar *18*. The fingering is reproduced from OE.

Bar *19*. At the beginning of this bar the more recent editions have the broken third F^2-$A\flat^2$. The arpeggio sign is not found in MS, FE or in Mikuli's edition (though it is in Madame Dubois's copy — see *Appendix* below).

Bar *20*. The fourth quaver in the left hand is given in both MS and FE as $E\flat^1$ alone, as in bar 12. Mikuli and recent editions have the third $E\flat^1$-$G\flat^1$.

Bar *21*. The tenth note in the treble is given in the original version as D^3 and not $E\flat\flat^3$, and the twentieth as G^3 and not $A\flat\flat^3$. But $E\flat\flat$ and $A\flat$ are here substitutes for $E\flat$ and $A\flat$, so that the notation as D and G is not correct.

Bars *23* and *24*. The last groups of thirds in these two bars raise problems. In bar 23 the demisemiquaver thirds, denoted by the sextuplet sign, might be most simply and naturally understood as two triplets; first because notes given as sextuplets in the rough draft and in MS (the figure is not found in FE) are as a rule two linked triplets, and secondly because the thirds so divided continue (at a quicker tempo) the pattern of the preceding semiquaver triplets. However, the question may be considered from another angle. Sometimes Chopin denotes by the figure 6 groups made up not of 2 x 3 notes but of 3 x 2 notes, and here he may have been basing himself not on the melodic line but on the basic rhythm of the preceding thirds, i.e. in the last group he may be continuing the triplet rhythm of the two preceding groups, but dividing each semiquaver into a pair of demisemiquavers. Such an interpretation seems to find further confirmation in the last group of bar 24. In the rough draft Chopin marked this group as 2 + 3 + 3. But the very fact that later on he changed this group into an octuplet consisting of notes of the same value implies that he viewed octuplet as consisting of even groups.

Bar 25. Over the third, fourth and fifth thirds OE gives the fingering 3 4 5, over the seventh and the eighth thirds $\frac{5}{1}\frac{3}{1}$, and further on over the following thirds the fingers 4 5 3, and for the twelfth and thirteenth thirds the fingering $\frac{4}{1}\frac{3}{1}$.

Bar 27. OE gives the third finger for the first $G\flat^3$ and the second finger for the C^3. Similarly the second finger is given for the first $D\flat^3$ and the second $A\flat^2$ in bar 28; in bar 30 the third finger is given for the $G\flat^3$ and the second finger for the $E\flat^3$.

Bar 31. The second finger for the grace note $D\flat^3$ and the fifth finger for the C^4 and the F^3 — the upper notes of the thirds — are taken from OE.' So is the first finger over the $F\flat^3$ (the lower note of the sixth third from the end of the bar). In the seventh third from the end, however, we have replaced OE's first finger by the second.

Bar 32. In the third third from the end of the bar MS and OE have no natural before the F^2, so that $F\flat$ should be read after the flat before the sixth third from the end. The natural is found both in FE and Mikuli.

Bars 35—36. The original version does not break the slur at the beginning of bar 35. In bar 36 MS does not have the fifth chord in the right hand, and the thirteenth, fourteenth and fifteenth chords are $G\flat^2\text{-}C^3\text{-}E\flat^3$, $G\flat^2\text{-}A\flat^2\text{-}F^3$, $E\flat^2\text{-}A\flat^2\text{-}C^3$. In the rough drafts this passage (except for the final eight bars) shows very great differences as compared with the final version. Special note should be taken of the original division of the group in the second half of bar 32 into $2+3+2$.

Bar 38. The third note from the end of the bar in the treble is given in MS, OE and the more recent editions as $F\flat^3$. The rough draft, however, has E^3, which we have restored, considering it as correct. It is the sharp fifth of the chord of the dominant seventh $A\flat\text{-}C\text{-}E\flat\text{-}G\flat$, which together with the G^2 continues the sequence of chromatic sixths in this passage. Furthermore, in an exactly similar context at bars 41—42 and 42—43, both MS and OE have E and not $F\flat$.

Bars 39—42. In MS the top notes of the triplets are not linked as semiquavers. FE was the first to single out these notes.

Bars 41 and 42. MS has as the fourth quaver in the left hand $E\flat^1\text{-}G\flat^1$ and not $C^1\text{-}G\flat^1$.

Bars 43—44. All the trills in these bars should begin on the upper note. In MS Chopin placed a flat before the $G\flat^1$ from which the second run in bar 44 starts (after the last trill), probably as a warning against playing G^1. However, the collected editions of Breitkopf & Härtel (Vol. X, No. 9) and Gebethner and Wolff (No. 375) have a natural here. In this run OE gives the first finger on the first, fourth and eighth notes, and the third finger on the sixth note. The fingering is thus as follows: 1 2 4 1 4 3 2 1 5 (see *Appendix* below).

Bars 45 and 46. In both these bars MS gives $B\flat\flat^2$ ($B\flat\flat^1$) and not $A\flat^2$ ($A\flat^1$) as the fifth note from the end of the bar. In the rough drafts $B\flat\flat^2$ is given in bar 45, and in bar 46 the last six notes are $E\flat^2\text{-}G\flat^1\text{-}G\flat^2$ and $A\flat^1\text{-}C^2\text{-}G\flat^1$.

Bars 47—48. MS begins the slur on the first note in the right hand of bar 47 and ends it on the first note of bar 48; it then starts a new slur on the next note. FE has the first of these slurs, but starts a second on the first note of bar 48 — i.e. the same note as the first slur ends on.

Bars 49—50. The fingering is reproduced from FE (see also *Appendix* below).

Bar 56. The fingering given here is to be found even in the rough draft. It is also given in FE.

Bars 56—57. FE adds a crotchet tail to the third note in the treble of bar 56 and to the fourth note of bar 57. The crotchet and quaver extensions are reproduced here and in bar 55 from Mikuli's edition. We have also added a quaver tail to the seventh note of bar 57 and linked as quavers the third and fifth notes of bars 56 and 57. Mikuli gives them separate tails.

Bar 59. In the rough draft and in MS the $B\flat^1$'s are not tied.

Bars 59—61. OE gives the first finger on the first and last semiquavers of bar 59, on the third and sixth of bar 60 and on the third, seventh and eleventh of bar 61; it gives the second finger on the semiquaver in bar 60.

Bar 63. The original version does not break the slur at the beginning of the bar.

Bars 66—67. Here we have retained the original notation. The following would, however, be more appropriate:

because we consider that the melody ends on the $D\flat^1$ on the fourth quaver of bar 67.

Appendix

Pedalling. MS marks no pedalling. We have reproduced the pedalling from FE. The collected edition of Breitkopf & Härtel marks two pedals in each bar up to and including bar 54 (with the exception of bars 25 and 26, where the pedal is given only for the first half of the bar, and bars 28 and 43, where three pedals are marked). This pedalling seems to us advisable.

The Library of the Conservatoire in Paris is in possession of the copy of the Berceuse (FE) which belonged to Madame Dubois, Chopin's pupil. In this copy there are signs and instructions added in pencil (possibly by Chopin himself), apparently in connection with the study of this work. In bar 13, beneath the last three semiquavers, is marked the fingering 1 1 2. The last note of the same bar, Gb^2, has been given an accent and tied to the Gb^2 at the beginning of the following bar. At the beginning of bar 19, before the third with the trill, an arpeggio sign has been inserted; this we have reproduced. In bar 25 the first finger is marked under the seventh, eighth, twelfth and thirteenth thirds. In bar 44, the fingers 1 3 are marked for the second trill, the first notes in the following run (Gb^1-Ab^1) are marked 2 1, and the three repeated Ab^2's are fingered 3 2 1. The last note of bar 48 and the first of bar 49 are to be played with the first finger, as are the second semiquavers of bars 59 and 60.

We should like to offer our sincere thanks to Monsieur Gérard Petitpierre of Paris, who has kindly supplied us with these data and has checked some other details of the Berceuse and Barcarolle in FE.

Barcarolle in F♯ major, op. 60

Abbreviations: MS — the autograph copy preserved in the Jagiellonian Library, Cracow (a reproduction was published by Polish Music Publications in Cracow, 1953). FE — the original French edition (Brandus et Cie, Paris, No. 4609). GE — the original German edition (Breitkopf & Härtel, Leipzig, No. 7545).

MS, though it contains many alterations and deletions, represents the final version, carefully provided with dynamic and agogic signs, pedalling, etc. FE is a very accurate copy of the version of MS. GE shows certain deviations in the dynamics, slurring, etc.

Bar 11. Mikuli, differing from FE and GE, gives $F\sharp$ and not $D\sharp$ as the first note of the last triplet in the left hand.

Bar 12. FE and GE start a new slur in the treble on the first note of the bar. MS has the slurring accepted in the present edition.

Bar 13. In contrast to bars 11 and 12, the tr here evidently means a mordent. Klindworth has changed the trill sign to an ordinary mordent.

Bar 18. In the bass, in contrast to bar 15, FE and Mikuli slur the quaver following crotchet not with the preceding but with the subsequent notes. MS has slurring in both these bars, and we have followed its example.

Bars 23 and 24. The fingering of the trills in thirds is given by Chopin in MS. From this it is obvious that the trills should begin on the upper notes. The trill in bar 26 should begin in the same way, especially since $F\sharp^2$ comes immediately before it (at the beginning of the bar). Towards the end of bar 24, GE has only $E\sharp^2$ as the grace note.

Bar 30. GE does not have the $D\sharp^2$ in the right hand in the third chord from the end of the bar.

As the ninth quaver in the left hand MS and Mikuli have only $D\sharp^1$.

Bar 31. The sign tr is certainly given instead of a mordent. In the corresponding bar 91 MS and FE have the usual mordent sign.

Bar 32. In the 10th and 11th chords in the right hand MS and GE add a B^2, as in the corresponding chords in the left hand. In view of the $dim.$, FE's version is more appropriate.

Bar 33. At the beginning of the bar FE and Mikuli have only B^1 as the grace note; MS and GE have B^1-$C\sharp^2$.

Bar 34. Here we have followed the original version. We recommend, however, that only the sixth $A\sharp^1$-$F\sharp^2$ be played in the right hand at the beginning of the bar, as at the beginning of the second half of the preceding bar, and by analogy with bar 16.

Bar 36. The fingering and the division of the passage between the two hands is found in the original version.

Bar 38. The original version does not add a quaver tail to the last note in this bar in either hand. Similarly, it has none in the right hand of bars 42 and 46.

Bar 39. GE does not tie the A^1 between bars 39 and 40.

Bars 41—42. MS does not tie $C\sharp^2$ — doubtless the result of a slip when moving from one staff to the next. Neither FE nor GE gives this tie, though Mikuli does. The corresponding B^1 in bars 45—46 is tied in MS and FE and by Mikuli; it is not tied in GE, which in this passage moves from one staff to the next, so that a similar slip may have occurred here.

Bar 48. Following Klindworth, we have separated the $C\sharp^1$ (the ninth quaver) from the lower voice in the right-hand part, and included it in the upper voice, by analogy with the corresponding $F\sharp^1$ in the preceding bar. FE gives $F\sharp$ and not $G\sharp$ as the third quaver in the right hand. Originally MS had $F\sharp$, but Chopin altered this to $G\sharp$. In the corresponding bar 59 MS again gives $F\sharp$, which this time, probably owing to an oversight, has not been corrected. In both these passages GE and Mikuli have $G\sharp$, which accords with the $G\sharp^1$ in the identical figuration in bars 49 and 60.

Bar 59. In GE, in the left hand, a crotchet tail is not added to the third note from the end of the bar, and the last note has an added upper octave $C\sharp$.

Bar 61. In MS, FE and GE the dotted crotchet $C\sharp^2$ is not tied to the following quaver.

Bar 64. MS and FE begin a new slur on the third beat of the bar in the right hand. The same notation is found in the corresponding bars 95 and 101. In the right hand of bar 99 MS and FE end the slur on the first chord on the third beat and start a new one on the following chord. This slurring marks the beginning of the motive. GE emphasizes the same motive in bars 68, 93, 95 and 101 in the same way. But as this slurring has not been carried out consistently in all the sources mentioned above, and as on the other hand the broad melodic line of the theme might easily suffer from being divided up, we consider that the slurring of longer passages is advisable.

B a r s *72—76*. The slurring is reproduced from GE. In MS and FE the whole of this passage is slurred, with a break at the beginning of bar 75.

B a r *73*. The original version does not tie the F^1's in the fourth and third quavers from the end of the bar, probably inadvertently. We have accepted Klindworth's version, which is similar to the corresponding phrase in the preceding bar.

B a r *76*. GE has $C\sharp$-$C\sharp$ as the first octave in the bass.

B a r *81*. As the tenth semiquaver in the right hand Mikuli has $B\sharp^2$ and not $C\sharp^3$, as also in the repetition of the same passage at the end of the bar.

B a r s *84—89*. In contrast to MS and FE and to its own version of bar 4 sqq. GE slurs only the five middle octaves in each figure in the bass. In these bars we give a different pedalling from that found in the original version. In GE the pedal is marked on the first beats of the bar; in MS and FE the pedalling partly agrees with GE's and partly with that of bar 4 sqq. where, however, we advise that it should remain as we have given it for bar 84 sqq.

B a r s *93—101*. The tying of the octaves or the chords at some points in this passage, as compared with the corresponding passage at bar 62 sqq. presents a certain problem. Both the octaves $F\sharp^2$-$F\sharp^3$ should certainly be tied between the sixth and seventh quavers in bar 98; MS, FE and Mikuli have this tie (which is missing in GE). The octaves $C\sharp^2$-$C\sharp^3$ at bars 94—95 are tied both in FE and in Mikuli's edition. The same applies to the corresponding $C\sharp^2$-$F\sharp\sharp^2$-$C\sharp^3$ at bars 100-101. The octaves $A\sharp^1$-$A\sharp^2$ in bars 96—97 and the octaves $C\sharp^2$-$C\sharp^3$ in bars 97—98 are not tied in MS, FE, GE or Mikuli's edition. The difference in these details was probably introduced deliberately in view of the different character of this repeated passage. It should be mentioned, however, that after bar 96 in MS Chopin began a new staff — on which, moreover, he made some corrections — and after bar 100 started the next page. An oversight in the marking of the ties is therefore not impossible. Klindworth has accepted the ties given by Mikuli, and we follow his example.

B a r *95*. The sixth quaver in the left hand is given in GE as B-$E\sharp^1$, and the third quaver of bar 96 as $G\sharp$-B-$E\sharp^1$.

B a r *97*. ME and FE clearly mark the lifting of the pedal on the third quaver, a new pedal on the

seventh lifted on the eighth, and then again a new one for the three last quavers.

B a r *100*. MS and FE link the fifth and sixth chords in the right hand with a separate slur.

B a r *101*. GE gives $B\flat$ instead of $A\sharp$ in the fifth chord, and A instead of $G\sharp\sharp$ in the sixth chord of the bar.

B a r *102*. The first chord in the bar in the left hand is notated in GE as a dotted crotchet. As the penultimate chord in the left hand GE has $B\sharp$-$D\sharp^1$-$F\sharp^1$-$G\sharp^1$. In MS, FE and Mikuli this chord is given as B-$D\sharp^1$-$F\sharp^1$-$A\sharp^1$. The $A\sharp^1$ leads to B^1 in the last chord in the bar. Over *tr* FE also indicates *ten.*

B a r *103*. GE marks *sempre forte*. In MS and FE this indication does not appear until bar 107. As the top note in the first chord on the third beat GE gives — apparently by mistake — $G\sharp^2$ instead of $F\sharp^2$.

B a r s *104—109*. MS, FE and GE give each of these bars a separate slur, starting on the first note in each. We begin the phrase on the second beat in these bars, as in bar 103 in the original version.

B a r *106*. The original notation has $C\sharp\sharp$ and not D in the chord on the third beat. This chord may be understood either as VII[7] in $C\sharp$ major with diminished seventh and flat third ($B\sharp$-D-$F\sharp$-A), resolving to $C\sharp$-$E\sharp$-$A\sharp$ (the $A\sharp$ being a sixth replacing the fifth), or as VII[7] with flat fifth in $A\sharp$ minor, resolving to $A\sharp$-$C\sharp$-$E\sharp$. Either case requires D and not $C\sharp\sharp$.

B a r *108*. In the original notation the second chord is first given with $B\flat$ instead of $A\sharp$, which in this chord is a harmony note (VII[7] in B minor).

B a r *110*. In that part of the run which descends from the top E^4, MS, FE and GE give no accidentals before the three E's. As a result there is some doubt as to whether these three notes should be read as $E\sharp$ or as E. The original notation certainly favours $E\sharp$, since the position of these three notes on the staff corresponds with that of the preceding E's with sharps, and they are not separated by E's with naturals. However, in view of the fact that the top E^4 has a natural, some editors have also added naturals before the subsequent E's. They considered that if Chopin wanted $E\sharp$ and not E in the latter part of the run, he should have restored the sharps before these last three E's. In fact, for safety's sake, either sharps or naturals should have been inserted. However, there was no necessity for this, and Chopin was not always so careful in his notation. On the other hand, it is more probable that in the descending part of the run all the components of the chord, i.e. $E\sharp$-G-B-D should appear in succession. The E in the first part of the run circumscribes, together with $C\sharp$, the $D\sharp$ which belongs to the chord. It also appears at the top in this character. At the end of the run, where the notes of the chord are no longer circumscribed, it is more natural to introduce all the harmony notes than to change one of them into a non-harmony note. Since the original notation — as has been shown — argues in favour of rather than against such an interpretation, we have accepted $E\sharp$ in the last three cases — backed moreover by the authority of Mikuli who, for certainty's sake, put a sharp before the first E after the top E^4. The original version indicates that the pedal should be lifted as early as the second quaver in the left hand. But with such pedalling the pedal note $F\sharp$ disappears too quickly, and in order to sustain it longer we advise that at the next change of pedal the so-called half-pedal should be applied.

Bar *113*. The fingers 1 4, given over the fifteenth and sixteenth as well as over the nineteenth and twentieth demisemiquavers, are found in MS and FE.

Bar *114*. The fingers 4 1 1 at the end of this bar are reproduced from MS and FE.

Bars *115—116*. We have reproduced GE's pedalling. MS and FE indicate that the pedal should be lifted only at the end of bar 115, and in bar 116 they have pedal signs under both the $C\sharp$ double octaves, lifting it on the following $F\sharp$'s.

DR LUDWIK BRONARSKI
Fribourg (Switzerland)

PROF. JÓZEF TURCZYŃSKI
Morges

FRYDERYK CHOPIN
COMPLETE WORKS

EDITIONS WITH POLISH, ENGLISH
FRENCH, GERMAN, HUNGARIAN, JAPANESE
RUSSIAN AND SPANISH TEXTS

HEAD OFFICE

POLSKIE WYDAWNICTWO MUZYCZNE

31-111 CRACOW, AL. KRASIŃSKIEGO 11A